FRENCH LEAVE

**Cliff Forshaw** has been a Royal Literary Fund Fellow at York and Hull Universities, twice a Hawthornden Writing Fellow, and held residencies at Djerrassi, California, and in France, Kyrgizstan, Romania, and Tasmania. He is also a painter.

*Also by Cliff Forshaw*

| | |
|---|---|
| RE:VERB | *(Broken Sleep Books, 2022)* |
| Satyr | *(Shoestring Press, 2017)* |
| Pilgrim Tongues | *(Wrecking Ball, 2015)* |
| Vandemonian | *(Arc, 2013)* |
| Trans | *(The Collective Press, Wales, 2005)* |

# Praise for *RE:VERB*

Part translation, part verse biography, but entirely a law unto itself, Cliff Forshaw's *RE:VERB* is a freewheeling *jeu d'esprit*, a cocktail of bad blood, 'gloomy lust and sanctimonious doom'. Rampaging from the beatific, foul-mouthed teenaged poet to the fulminations of *Une saison en enfer* and the crucible of Africa, *RE:VERB* is a *chasse spirituelle* of sortilege and thaumaturgy, delivered with exquisite verve and oomph. Could Rimbaud read it himself, he would surely be moved to the same outburst he reserved for reminders of his work — 'Absurd, ridiculous, disgusting.'

— David Wheatley

These poems reflect the fiercely independent spirit which characterised Arthur Rimbaud in all the phases of his short, turbulent life. In tightly-structured verse and vigorous, earthy diction, Cliff Forshaw lets the poet tell his own story, but in counterpoint with other voices and characters who see him through the filter of his masks as merchant, explorer and ethnographer. Drawing on documents and letters, but wearing his research lightly, Forshaw unravels the poet's tangled adventures in Africa, Asia and elsewhere with welcome incisiveness. His colourful poems of place and mood also illuminate Rimbaud's inner life, and leave us with some intriguing clues as to why the brilliant *poète maudit* gave up his vocation and 'donned the grotesque finery of trade'.

— Carol Rumens

# French Leave
# Versions & Perversions

*Cliff Forshaw*

Broken Sleep Books

ISBN: 978-1-915760-16-6



Cover designed by Aaron Kent

Edited & Typeset by Aaron Kent

Broken Sleep Books Ltd
Rhydwen
Talgarreg
Ceredigion
SA44 4HB

Broken Sleep Books Ltd
Fair View
St Georges Road
Cornwall
PL26 7YH

# *Contents*

*Take French leave*: depart or act without having permission or giving notice. ***Concise Oxford Dictionary***

For friends among the living
and masters echoing from the dead.
We'll always have Paris.

## *Gautier's Theory of Art*

*after Théophile Gautier (1811-72)*

The work that shines out best
loves forms that are tough and tight,
that tantalise and test,
as you shape up for the fight.

No arbitrary constraints:
Oulipian rules for prose,
or music, verse and paint,
just get up the public's nose.

Make poems keep their beat,
lose the boots that hobble you.
– You'll never find your feet
in a badly-cobbled shoe.

*A sculptor's work in clay*
*invites its own decay;*
*his mind gives way to play*
*while his thumb rubs all away.*

Struggle with hard marble,
some oddly glittering stone
from Kandahar or Kabul:
work onyx, turquoise, bone.

Borrow from ancient masters
the bronze that outlasts time;
view fame and loss, disaster,
from Parnassus in perfect rhyme.

With a hand both sure and delicate
(where ancients led you follow):
you take a vein of agate,
cut a profile of Apollo.

> *Write and paint if you must,*
> *but only an art that's robust*
> *can, like a tyrant's bust,*
> *survive the city's dust.*

The gods themselves all die;
let the poet take his pains,
when all around him lies,
so his brassy verse remains.

Hammer! Chisel! Plane!
Take the fight to stone.
To deal with *stuff*'s what's sane;
leave concepts well alone.

## *Gautier's Farewell to Poetry*

*two variations after Théophile Gautier*

### 1.

Come, fallen angel, and let your pink wings close;
Lose the white robe; turn off your rays of gold.
High time to quit the sky; it's feeling old.
End like the shooting star; fall into prose.

Your bird-like feet must learn to tread the ground.
You've flown enough. No need to any more.
Don't harp on the music you played and how you soared.
Lock it in your heart. Don't make a sound.

Sky-child, your song's divine, but sung in vain:
They wouldn't understand your sweet Enochian.
Their ears are deaf to your ancient artifice.

But, before you go, my blue-eyed guardian,
Seek out the pale one whom I love, and press
Upon her brow, one long, last farewell kiss.

## 2.

It's time to drop the rebel angel act.
It's getting hard for you to rock that black:
the leather and shades – that look's not coming back.
It's hard to say this now with any tact,

but your boho aesthetic no longer shocks, been worked
to death by generations of sullen kids.
Remember why you first did those things you did.
Love or anger? Then why you became a jerk.

And here, the cliché – reversed – 's almost true:
it really isn't me, but the likes of you.
Get real. It's over. Leave poetry to the Dead.

You played at being Byron, Rimbaud. Kidded
no one, though you took yourself so seriously:
one eye on the mirror, your verses' true dedicatee.

# *Shadowed*

*two variations on "El Desdichado" by Gérard de Nerval (1808-55)*

*Je suis le ténébreux, – le veuf, – l'inconsolé*

## 1. Device Emblazoned Upon a Lute

Shadowed, widower, scion of an ancient line,
My domain now lost, withered to a ruined folly.
My only star is dead and that rising sign
Upon my lute is the black sun of Melancholy.

You who consoled me, who lightened my despair,
Bring to the night of my tomb Posilipo, the wine-
Dark sea, the flower which chased away my cares,
And the arbour where the rose entwines with the vine.

Eros? Apollo? With whose myth was my blood mixed?
My brow is still scorched from the kiss of that dark queen.
I've dreamed where the Siren swims in her marine

Caverns. Twice, I've won my way across the Styx,
Harmonising as I strummed the lyre's now slackening strings
The sighs of saints and sprites, the hum of brittle wings.

## 2. Bloozer

Good school. Natch. Got kicked out.
Trouble in the City. Did my time.
Trust-fund once, didn't trust trustees,
the rest I blew all on my own.

My feet, my thumb, got me this far.
Bootsoles, truck-stops, passing cars.
And now all I've got left's this ten-buck
standby for the hocked guitar

(Mama's birthday gift I learned upon):
warped neck, fret-buzz, slips in and out of tune,
left out too long, I guess, in northern rain,
in upland sleet, those months in deep-south sun.

But it busks, plays fast and, hey, the slide's real loose.
Things hit. With Fate expect no truce.
Too much devilment; forgot what sounds like Heaven;
we're talking flattened fifth and minor seventh.

I followed my heart through that sound-hole.
Been more than once through fire, highwater, Hell.
This wooden box is noisier than the other one,
and rings as clear as any churchyard bell.

The trick's to add the words which tell no lies,
put lyrics to a bottle skidding wires.
If I'm a loser, then let me loose to lose.
Augment, suspend, diminish, slide and bend

that long leaning note. At last no need to fret!
I'll let Disaster be my Muse!
Bring it on. I'm already walking
while you're still talking talking blues.

# *Myrtho*

*a version after Gérard de Nerval and a variation*

## 1.

I think of you, my Myrtho – sly sorceress
haloed by Posilipo's molten light:
you wear a volcano for a crown, brow bright,
tresses burnished like lava braiding ash.

I took your proffered cup and I looked up
to catch the liquid lightning of your eye.
Today, I pray at Dionysos' – here Bacchus' – shrine;
so, born-again, Muse-suckled, my soul stays Greek.

I now know why the mountain shrugs and cracks
– you brushed it with your fleeting foot. It gapes
to unmake the world; all is acrid, smoke-thick, cloaked.

Some Norman duke has broken all your clay gods open
and, under Virgil's laurel, I have seen
the pale hydrangea married to the myrtle's green.

## 2.

*"La terre bouge, elle m'inspire aucune confiance": overheard, rough-sleeper, Salle d'Attente, Gare du Nord, 1973*

Druidical under oaks, ash-dripping elms:
weird sorceress, always volcano-crowned...
I looked into your blackened bowl and saw
day trembling on the edge, then drank that fire.

To some, your gods were shattered earthenware,
mere shards, but I see your rubble everywhere;
and what was cracked was what you broke.

I'd always felt you close, knew you'd snaked right through
to broker emptiness on once solid ground.

Earth-sick. The after-shocks came long and huge.
For months the day's been coughing up a pall,
fire waltzing at its hem. *La terre bouge*
(so thick and black) – the village chokes. Earth moves,
it inspires me with no confidence, no confidence at all.

# *Vin Voudou*

*two variations on "Sed non satiata" by Charles Baudelaire (1821-67)*

## 1. Vendange d'outre-mer

Odd goddess, whose skin's a smoky musk
still redolent of opium and Havana.
You may be some obi-man's opus, some savannah
saviour's ju-ju, or child of the Bayou dusk.

Forget your *Grands*, your *Premiers Crus*, your *Nuits*;
for *tenue*, what lasts long on my tongue's your mouth.
*You* are my full-bodied beaker of the South;
you slake, yet provoke thirst better than any Burgundy.

I note the rich *robe*, as you hold me with your eyes:
the worm goes through the cork, I'm mesmerised
to breathe the *botánica*'s bouquet and, as I taste

your voodoo vin *gris-gris*, too late, I'm lost;
my palate echoes with *santería*; head
with your *blanc de noirs*, those lives I never led.

**2. Déjà-bu**

No wine is fine enough; no drug can do
the tricks you (turn and) do, my wine-dark sea,
my nest of mermaids, my girl in every port,
the witchy Circe of this odyssey
who dulls all thoughts of fine Penelope.
My mind's your glass. You take my stem and twirl.
I'm half a world away: moly, oily swirls
of sea-serpents, sargassos. Shipwrecked, all at sea,

washed up on some calypygian Aphrodite's
shore, whose wily Calypso I discover to be you.
Have we lived and loved in other lives?
You always my stormy siren. Me, *saoul*
...drunk, rudderless, compass-less, (compassionless
for that good – still faithful? – wife). Lost. Déjà-bu.

# *Synaesthesia*

*variations on Baudelaire's "Correspondences"*

## 1.

So, you say Nature's a living temple whose columns
writhe to let a muddled phrase break free?
Weird wood! I can see we're watched from every tree.
Whorls on the boughs mouth out to us. The solemn

silence writes scripts to bark. And in the distance,
wavelength goes indigo, as vast as night,
runs clear as ice-melt, pours out its solace in light.
Wherever you look, it's all utterance. Or could be.

A fragrance resonates with spring; think fresh
showers, wild flower meadows. Others unstopper dusk:
rich and dark, they linger, heavy as flesh

which knows velvet and amber, benjamin and musk.
You go beyond the quiddity of things;
taste the jazzy keys of colour; hear perfumes sing.

## 2.

Sometimes the world seems a living temple.
You move through side chapels, beady-eyed
by wise and symbolic birds, their calls
echo in arches, high stained windows; a shaft
of light haloes the earth around your feet.
You fall through the taste of nut and worm,
mulch, leaf-rot, incoming weather,
what's borne on air, picking up the spectrum
of insect broadcast. Everything sharpens:

constellations of pollen motes; you zoom
to the focus of one tiny brain-buzz in the billions,
magnetic hair or sat-nav shell conductivity.
Banded by ions, tuned to the radio of sun and dark,
the world turns on the pin-point of a gnat.

# *In Another Life*

*after Baudelaire's "La Vie antérieure"*

I lived an age cambered under vast arches:
the walls were burnished each evening by disks
of mosaic gold; sun molten in the sea as dusk
dug huge basalt caverns through my porches.

As long swells rolled in under moody skies,
the solemn elemental diapason began.
Across the slow boom of the horizon,
colour bled rich harmonies into my eyes.

I lived there enveloped in voluptuous calm,
soothed by the sound of endless falling waves,
the attentive hands of perfumed, naked slaves

who were tasked, with fragrant oils and palms,
to fan my brow, nuance that subtle anguish,
the sadness I cultivated as I languished.

# *The Tomb of Charles Baudelaire*

*after Stéphane Mallarmé (1842-98)*

A buried temple, sunk in the sewer's dark:
that sepulchral mouth, slobbering night-soil and rubies,
reveals a horrible god – dog-headed Anubis,
snout poking, already primed with a savage bark.

Take the municipal gas-light's wick and twist
to wipe from night your day of gaffes and wrecks.
A haggard vision glows: immortal sex
lit by street-lamps, flitting into mist.

In cities where evening is banished, what dry leaves
can serve as votive flame for the woman who weaves
vain wreathes against Baudelaire's cold marble?

Though veiled, there's a shiver to cover his absence still
as a Shade, guardian angel of poison, garbles
a verse about perfume that enchants to kill.

## *The Tomb of Edgar Allan Poe*

*after Mallarmé*

Eternity has wrought the final change
– he has become himself, still holding his blade
against the age's throat. He will not fade;
he saw Death's victory, made it newly strange.

As when the angel came; the mob once heard
him purify their worn-down tribal words.
Drunk, their tongues all thick, they gibbered, slurred;
cast out his spells, the truths they found absurd.

Out of hostile soil and cloud, comes grief
from which to try to sculpt a bas-relief
to ornament the dazzling tomb of Poe.

This calm block, fallen from unknown disaster,
may mark the bounds, where none beyond dare go
to the black flights of Blasphemy, the forever after.

## *The Tomb of Paul Verlaine*

*after Mallarmé*

This dark rolling stone who blamed the wind
could never pause for even pious hands
and, though sympathetic to the human wound,
rolled on to find and fill his fateful ground.

Here, almost always if the ring-dove coos,
this cloudy wake obscures the many folds
where stars have ripened for darkly future fields
and sparks reveal the gathering silvered crowds.

Who searches for the solitary leaps and bounds
till now beyond our far-gone vagabond?
No naïve surprise at what has come to pass.
– Verlaine? Verlaine? He's hidden in the grass.

Undrinking lips, his chest unmoved by breath.
Our shallow streams all calumnised by death.

## *Low*

*after "Spleen" by Paul Verlaine (1844–96)*

The roses all around so red,
The ivy all around so black.

You merely move your lovely head
And all my fears come flooding back.

Too blue, too tender was that sky,
The air too soft, the sea too green.

I always feared, though not sure why,
Some dreadful thing as yet unseen.

I am so tired of these bouquets,
Of all this endless nature too.

I'm bored of all these country days.
Bored of everything ...but you.

## *Overheard*

*after Verlaine's "Colloque sentimental"*

I saw, in the lonely frozen park,
two spectres in the gathering dark.

Their lips seemed thin, their eyes quite dead.
– I caught a little of what they said.

There in the lonely frozen park,
I heard one ghostly form remark

how momentous their love had been.
"Do you still think of me? Still dream?

Do you still tremble at my name?"
– "No, that's long gone. We're not the same."

"Such times of irreplaceable bliss
when our lips met!" – "It was just a kiss…"

"Our sky was vast. And our hope too!"
– "Long gone, just like the sky's brief blue."

The park was still. There were no birds.
Now only night would hear their words.

## *Vowels*

*after Arthur Rimbaud (1854-91)*

A – black, E – white, I – red, U – green, O – blue: vowels.
Some day I'll explain your occult origins.
A, black corset of glittering flies, diamond skins
buzzing above the cruel stench of voided bowels;

gulfs of shadow. E, white-outs of steam, canvas tents,
sharp glacier spears, white kings, iceberg tips.
I, purples, spat blood, the twist of pretty lips
gashed in anger or drunkenly penitent.

U, cycles, the green seas which never cease,
the sleeping beasts' spread paws, the wrinkled peace
on the shaman's brow, the spectral song which never dies.

And O: the supreme trumpet, full of strange harmonies;
silences crossed by angels, warping the world's eddies.
O, Omega, the ultra-violet of God's eyes.

## *Lascaux*

*impromptu on a theme from Rimbaud*

Fireberry budded early on our tribe's tongue:
sparked flint, cave-cooled to, oh listen to it... sound
echoing between our ears, our minds, we ground,
learned to beer-gurgle our powdered flowers, sang.
Later in the long night's flicker, spat red through fingers,
added our children to the forest of hands.

We learn by spilling life from the throat of things to keep
them running forever across our stony, what was it? Mind?
Or is it all just our green ground? Stab, dribble, spit.
Everything gives its drip or spark. Now sharpen, split and knap.

So, here is yellow. See there is blue. We do sunflower, woad.
Up there, everything comes together in indigo light.
Down here, daub walls. One day we'll set it all down right:
those things we keep apart. Else, we end, we end in mud.

# *Looking Back Down the Road*

*loosely after Rimbaud's "Au Cabaret-Vert" and "Ma Bohème"*

## 1. Taking Off

Those days I'd split without a second's thought. Hit the road.
Just take off. At seventeen, I'd tramp for miles, hitch a ride
no place special. Leather jacket like a scarred second hide.
Signposts for sonnets, truckers' long-load tales for odes.

Service stations, greasy spoons, thumbing cars, cars, cars.
Wind finding new holes in the knees and arse of my strides.
Blacktop, humming rubber, Autobahn-piste-strada.
Crashed out dead in graveyards, dossing under skidding stars.

Sat at the roadside, under creaking trees, the huge race
of clouds. September nights, dew sparkling my face.
Swigging lager from a stolen can: clean, cold, sharp.

Conjuring visions from shadows. Hidden in secret places,
I'd twist feet up close to my heart, pluck the laces
of my wounded boots, entire body turned to *(canned music)* – ***Harp***.

## 2. At the Green Café, 5pm

A full week on back roads, dusty mountain tracks.
Old Chinese canvas shoes were shagged-out shreds.
I hobbled into this one-camel town, back
of beyond, saw the green sign, smelled fresh baked bread.

Splashed face at the pipe, dragged fingers through hair.
Inside this girl looked up – great tits – cracked me a smile;
flicked a rag over the green oil-cloth, dusted off a chair.
I stretched out my legs, took in the shiny painted tiles.

She looked good around the eyes, not shy at any rate.
Fetched slabs of bread, butter, thick folds
of home-smoked ham on a brightly-coloured plate.

Pink and white – delicious, garlicky. For something cold,
she foamed up this huge mug. Getting too late
for the border, a quirky ray of sun turning beer to gold.

# *The Dirtied Heart*

*after Rimbaud's "Le Cœur volé", also known as" Le Cœur du pitre"*

My sea-sick heart is slobbering at the poop,
My tobacco-spattered heart.
Over it, they spurt their filthy soup!
My dirtied heart is slobbering at the poop,
Taking the jibes of that smirking troop
– Too-matey matelots who burp and fart.
My dirtied heart is slobbering at the poop,
My tobacco-spattered heart.

The Galley is daubed with marauding pricks,
The cock-jokes in the Head are depraved.
The graffiti in the gangway makes me sick,
Likewise those barrack-room pricks.
O magical abracadabra of the wave,
Take my heart, wash it and save
It from the barrack-room pricks,
The cock-jokes of the depraved.

When they've spat their quids out on the deck
How shall I act, my sea-sick heart?
Those Bacchic lads are up for the crack,
They've already spat out their quids on the deck.
I'm sick to my stomach, ready to retch,
Puke up their dirty jokes, their filthy folk art.
Now they've spat their quids out on the deck,
How shall I act, O sea-sick heart?

# *A Mixed Bunch of Poet's Flowers*

*after Rimbaud's "Ce qu'on dit au poète à propos de fleurs"*

**Lilies**

On the Poet's list one bloom is top,
For trembling by the topaz seas:
O Lily, long the poet's prop,
O enema of ecstasies!

But in this age of sago pud
And heavy labour on the farm,
Your lilies grow from *soul*, not mud,
Exuding an oddly pious charm.

Your lines are gilded with lilies, lilies,
Which, day-to-day, are rarely seen.
Farm-folk will find such verses silly:
Why do they *tremble*? So what's that *mean*?

When the Poet takes a shower,
His shirt's on the line with his meagre kit:
A fluttering common or garden flower,
With yellow deodorant-stained armpits.

## Roses

And if the Poet decides on roses?
He pens them red, inflated, blown.
O laurel stem! The question posed is:
Where on earth are such roses grown?

The Poet snows his roses down:
In bloody great red drifts they lie.
– Imagine the snow-red rosy ground!
*Red* snow? Red mists *this* reader's eye.

French veg is ugly, gnarly, crabby
– Pissed on by weasels, rats and hounds.
French verse abhors the low-down shabby
Tubers prised from stony ground.

O Great White Hunter in the wild,
Tracking prey through the Fields of Pan,
You paint yourself as Nature's Child
But botanic ignorance reveals the man.

Sometimes even exotic species
Can't outweird your mythical blooms:
Stuff that feeds on unicorn faeces,
Or craves the shade of Pharoahs' tombs.

Your verse turns over good French earth,
And weeds out all its native plants.
The poet's now a floral flirt
Wearing orchidaceous fancy pants.

## Green Shoots of Recovery

I know you're taken by the tropics,
But try to be more down-to-earth.
Add economics to your topics:
Think what those foreign fields are worth!

Time now to praise the great plantations
– Sugar, cotton, coffee, tea.
No need for slavish imitations
Of do-gooder eco pieties

– Screw them and their sanctimony;
Freedom means the Market's free.
What's truly holy is the money.
The freshest growth is GNP.

The future's here and tapping rubber
For Mackintosh's waterproofs.
The whale at least gives up its blubber;
You blub liberally but stay aloof.

Your antique mythic scenery's
(Asphodels gathered by Venus and Cupid)
Just creaky stage machinery.
It's all about the economy, stupid!

Lose the amaranths, such plants
Obscure just what is really plain.
Your mystic visions are worn-out, pants.
The drowsy poppy's for killing pain.

Tradesman! Colonist or Medium!
Your rhymes now gutter pink and white.
Forget your midnight oily tedium:
Turn on the bud of electric light!

Sing of useful growing profits,
Laud workers set to tasks like ants.
Forget the floral; be the prophet;
Hymn the blooming industrial plant!

Our seasons now have all grown hellish.
This is what the future's for.
Just describe it, don't embellish,
The flowery rhetoric's a bore.

The future's bright, now listen to it:
Electric wires begin to hum,
Those old-style Poets were deaf and blew it;
Think four-stroke metre and banged oil drum.

From your dark poems, new lights must rise:
Illuminate those reds, blues, greens;
Pin swarms of acetylene butterflies;
Write of things as yet unseen.

*La Ville Lumière* has banished night:
– No Baudelairean Flowers of Evil –
It's time to rhyme potato blight
With noble rot and the flour weevil.

Lose the muse of bucolic lies,
The dawn's new chorus trills alarms
As other horrible workers rise
To man the aisles at factory farms.

Progress means increasing yields.
Irrigation! Drain what's sodden!
Bogs and deserts turned to fields!
One must be absolutely modern!

# *Toad*

*after "Le Crapaud" by Tristan Corbière (1845–75)*

Listen! There's a song this airless night.
See that slice of shiny tin? Moonlight,
a cut-out backdrop of deep green dark.

A song: its vibrely creaky echo
from the rockery beyond the decking.
It's shut its gob. Let's have a dekko!

Toad! Why are you so scared of me?
I'm your faithful servant. Don't you know it?
Just look at him: a baldy, wingless poet.
Junk-dump nightingale. Singing… horribly.

Well, is it really such an awful croak?
Can't you see the bright glint in his eye?
No? He's buggered off, crawled beneath his rock.
Old toady-boyo's really me – Okey-Doke.

*Goodbye!*

## *Lullabye-bye*

*a sort of Rondel for After, after Tristan Corbière; from "Rondels pour après"*

It's getting dark, child, stealer of sparks.
There are no more nights. There are no more days.
Sleep… waiting for those girls who'd remark
now how they'd "Never!", then how they'd "Always!"

Do you hear their steps? So light on their little feet.
How love has wings, flies and sings like the lark.
It's getting dark, child, stealer of sparks.

Do you hear their voices? The cellar's deaf and black.
Sleep as light as the trees snug in their bark.
Your friends, the bears, they won't be coming back
or hurling rocks at the ladies in the park.
It's getting dark, child, stealer of sparks.

## *Friends with Benefits*

*after 'À une camarade' by Tristan Corbière (additions by B.Dylan)*

Got your number. No need to be so coy.
What is it that you want from me exactly?
I'm no adoring little cute toy-boy.
Want me to worship you? ...Like you did me?

I loved you... like a peeling lizard loves
the sun which bakes its sleep. Love flutters wings,
a swan or swallow, the shadow of a dove...
Get it out my light! That tatty batty thing!

Love is nought, and when the serve's returned,
he's aced; it's all a racket for this loser.
As a good-for-nothing, he's got talent to burn.
Early doors, a lunchtime legend in his boozer.

Is Love a thingummy, trinket, knick-knack, bauble?
You can mend a broken vase with glue,
and, if it's plaster – or plastic – but maybe not marble,
stick a statuette back together, too.

But not this guy! Once broken he stays unstuck.
We're knocking on Heaven's door. Don't boot it open.
On the other side, our Eden's turned to muck;
best keep the skin on our apple green, unbroken.

What have I done to you? And you to me?
Not much. Perhaps the very reason why
we both forget who kicked off first. Not easy
to walk, or stay and shout, "Fffffff off and die!"

We're both still tangled up in blue, for sure,
though I always seem to come out worse
– one wanting less, then wanting so much more;
or vicey-versa, I'm still perversely cursed.

It seems our Love is calling it a day.
Would *friends with benefits* maybe work for you?
Time to bite our tongues. What d'ye say?
(And don't believe those lies! 'Specially if they're true!)

Let's not badmouth – play nice with one another.
We get the giggles after ripping off strips of flesh:
that Beatrice 'n' Benny-Dick act's a knackering bother
              – and still recalls your lovely laugh when we were fresh.

## *Pierrot Impromptu*

*improvisation on "Pierrot pendu" by Tristan Corbière*

Woman is a pill
You don't know how to sugar.
She takes you for a fool.
You feel a silly bugger.

She stoops to ridicule
Your expressions of desire,
Mocks your *inappropriate tool*
– By which (I think) she means my lyre.

## *Pages Ripped from a Pierrot's Phrase Book*

*fragments after "Locutions des Pierrots" by Jules Laforgue (1860-87)*

**Page I** *[Les mares de vos yeux aux joncs de cils]*

When will those pools with their bull-rush lashes
– I refer, O languid Lady, to your peerless eyes –
Reflect my equally peerless passion,
And catch my soul's moon-rise?

For the best part of an hour now
I've drunk your harshness up.
My simple heart is sad and cowed
And as meek as a Labrador pup.

Now, this should really be a doddle,
But, darling, it simply isn't nice:
You're no one's idea of a super-model
So don't act like you're made of ice.

**Page III** *[Ah! sans Lune, quelles nuits blanches]*

The moonless nights are sleepless too,
But the nightmares get creative.
Do you think those swans are me and you?
Do you think we might go native?

I'm only here because I care,
But I'm starting to see double.
I'm only catching solid air,
And fishing where the water's troubled.

Tell me now before I'm lost
About that pretty circumflex;
That's the arch where I'm blessed and crossed,
Puzzling the secret of your sex.

**Page VIII** *[Ah! tout le long du cœur]*

Ah! The whole heart long,
We've heard that same old, same old song.
Time to call time; go bang that gong
To end Love's lyric, and rhyme life's pong.

And now? So did I hurt you
While my sobs were just for show?
It's hard to believe you didn't know.
The signs were all there. Didn't they alert you?

Love sends us all quite soppily loopy
With its perfumes and dainty flowers;
You sip quaint thin tisanes for hours,
While I cook up something goatily soupy.

**Page XII** *[Encore un livre; ô nostalgies]*

Another book: O nostalgia-fest,
Far from the boorish crowd (so brash!).
No claps, no mucky, brassy cash,
None of your lingo's underdressed second-best.

Another pierrot kicks the bucket,
Dead of chronic orphantitis;
His dandy heart was, like most writer's,
A luminary Lunary in a jokey jacket.

The gods have gone, and Life's a bore.
The Daily Slog is getting worse.
I've done my time. This job's a curse.
Gimme the All-in, All-time Sinecure!

## *Mooning*

*loosely after Jules Laforgue's "Clair de lune"*

To think I'll never live upon that astral rock's
a nasty smack – a sudden epigastral shock.

All for you, O moon, as you gently slide
through the midsummer mimickry of eventide.

And as you roll, dismasted, look down on me
from the rollicking of the clouds' high seas.

O baptismal font in the sky's great roof,
dip my poor soul. Make it waterproof!

I'm a ship deceived by the wreckers' light;
a cold-night Icarus, lunatic and lost in flight.

Mme. Presidente, eye sterile as suicide,
convene this AGM of the hopelessly weak and tired.

Your icy skull now mocks the bald inanities
of our incurably pettydantic bureaucracies.

Pill of the ultimate unalarmed buttonless snooze,
we sip at your most potent over-proof booze.

O Diana, huntress, with your dress so Doric,
your arrows shoot us down. Alas, poor Yoricks!

Inoculate these wingless beings who are so earthbound,
for their hearts remain innocent and, mostly, sound.

O Planet washed by nameless floods, I pray:
pour down your chaste anti-inflammatory rays

upon my sheets, so I may wash my hands
of life in this so sadly sublunary land.

# *Bats*

*after Jules Laforgue's "Les chauves-souris"*

The bells are ringing wildly out
    From the convent of the Carmelites,
    In fact they sound quite mad tonight.
Let's find out what it's all about.

In the rafters' dust, weird things
    Are agitating through the slats:
    A hectic nest of baby bats
Twitching quaint old-fashioned wings.

Soon they'll go out on their sorties,
    Mosquito-hunting in the dank
    Along the night-time river bank
Where, earlier, women drubbed their laundry.

Banal yet cosmically sublime,
    The sunsets here can seem quite lonely,
    With shows put on for themselves only
And curtain up is bang on time.

Earth doesn't care if I'm here or absent:
    And hasn't since this planet drifted
    Through ignorant aeons as gas got sifted
Into skies one might describe as *god-sent*.

The sky will still be up itself
    When I no longer shout "Encore!"
    When it's not wanted any more
And its dusty gems are stored on the shelf.

And it would all be just OK
    If this boho nobody, dull as the rest,
    Had not yet bothered to exist,
Or taken my name for soubriquet.

## *Complaint of the Pianos Heard in the Comfortable Quarters*

*after Jules Laforgue's "Complainte des pianos qu'on entend dans les quartiers aisés"*

Lead those tasteful, cultured, sensitive souls,
Pianos, pianos, in the leafy quarters,
Through their first evening chaste and coatless strolls
To the highly-strung laments their nerves have tautened.

What do they dream of, these girls, bored in their cells
By scales, the eternally returning ritournelles?

– Schoolyards of dimming lights,
Sleepless dormitory Christs!

*"Off you go and leave us here.*
*You leave us here and off you go.*
*We pin up, brush out our hair,*
*Needle samplers; sew, sew, sew."*

Pretty? Plain? Wise? Sad? And still so pure?
Not bothered – or want the world and want it now?
If still virgin, nobly wounded, that's for sure,
And knowing what sunset had the whitest vow.

Each girl sleeping tight in her space,
Dreaming – of what? Of heroes or lace?

The hearts imprisoned
Through long, long seasons.

*"Off you go and leave us lonely.*
*You leave us lonely and off you go.*
*Grey convents, our breasts crossed only*
*By our own arms, as the choir now drowns our solos."*

One day, each found her Being's fatal key.
Psst! Look how ceaseless heredity
Works the carnival of our avenues
– Boarding schools, theatres, columns of news.

Enough of these eternal ritournelles,
Life is real and full of criminals.

– "Now the curtains are being drawn;
Who dares enter where houses yawn?"

*"You'll go away and leave us planted.*
*You'll leave us planted and go away.*
*Those roses we so deeply wanted*
*Are gone forever and a day."*

He'll be back and it's you who'll catch the blame,
You sad fiancées, engaged to endless regret,
Your smug spoilt hearts remain so much the same
As fashion exacts its incremental debt.

To die? Or work the needle – homilies
For your dowry and the wheedling family.

– "Never! Never! No!
What could you ever know?"

*"Off you go and leave us lonely.*
*You leave us lonely and off you go.*
*But you'll come back to us, here so lowly,*
*Cure our sickness. Is that not so?"*

It's true. Ideals are why they go astray:
The boho vine's best grown in leafy quarters.
That's life; but the whiskery aqua vitae, they say,
's best served not straight, but cut with baptismal water.

Stick at scales; soon you'll learn well
To play more nuanced ritournelles.

– "One pillow, ah, that's all.
And the same old, same old wall."

*"Off you go and leave us here.*
*You leave us here and off you go.*
*Masses grow longer, instill the fear*
*Of dropping off and boring God.*
*The months of Sundays, whole Mondays of laundry,*
*Years darning odd socks*
*...These endless evenings we sew."*

## *Propitiatory Complaint to the Thoughtless*

*loosely after Jules Laforgue's "Complainte propitiatoire à l'Inconscient"*
*To Aditi, Mother of the Vedic gods*

Thy Law be Law because it's Right,
down to the letter, shining Light!

*Her indoors*: should I worship, kneel and grovel?
Or Schadenfreudilly relish her every pain?
Swears she'd stay, even living in a hovel.
Next thing, my loss is some other guy's gain.

Let Thy thoughtless Will be done,
till all Eternity's been and gone.

Could die from the merest touch of Eucharist wafer,
the organ's tortured, guts all ripped apart;
I'm squatting under bright stained glass, a loafer
with skinny Jesus crucifixing my heart.

In Holy Communion may we find
daily wisdom, peace of mind.

Cities shifted, crossed by my shed blood;
a world-wide Easter blessed beyond Sin's wages;
to die upon the Mount for Mankind's good;
borne on their shoulders for endless Golden Ages.

Forgive us our trespasses, hands we've bitten,
what's done to what's not yet been written.

To crucify the Infinite in small
– a tiny canvas – you say the Ideal stays dumb.
To capture Man, you need The Whole, The All.
How will you master that, my clever chum?

Don't work: what you think and what you've thunk.
Your brain's best use: just getting drunk.

You're drifting daftly on a raft. And then?
All *Then* is gone. Along with *When*. Amen.
Amen.

## *Complaint of this Good Moon*

*loosely after Jules Laforgue's "Complainte de cette bonne lune"*

*Listen to the stars:*

In the lap of those odd gods:
o, there we dance, o, there we dance
(toe-tap, toe-tap, toe-tap, we prance)
mapping the heavens, so lightly shod,
in our trances, in our trances.

– There, look! Play nice, O Lady Moon:
the dance awaits. Just call the tune!
Sedate works well, nothing reckless;
these golden suns will be your necklace.

I'm not some ashy Cinderella.
Just don't do grate-ful. So, "*Ciao, Bella!*"
Meanwhile I have, and much prefer,
the orb my sister lends me to wear.

– Forget the stars. You own the stage.
Come join the cabaret... Turn heads.
Celeb? You're cooler than any star. *Drop-dead*
*gorgeous*. Snapped, papped, all the rage.

Well, thanks, I chew my crummy crust
and hear the crackle, going bust.

– That tinnitus within your ears
is just the music of the spheres.

Wash out your mouth, then shut your gob!
I've got my eye on these back-alleys,
their toughs and hussies, the chavvy mob.

– You floury May Queen or silly moo?
Our Lady of the Pissed-Up Crowd,
card-sharps, werewolves, that Bogeyman's crew,
itching tom-cats to rut out loud.
        You, you, you... cuckoo!

*Exeunt the stars. Silence of the spheres.*        *One hears:*

                Under the roof,
                all warp and woof,
        there we dance, there we dance.
                Under the roof,
                all warp and woof,
        there, prance in a trance,
                we dance, we dance.

# *Complaint of the Barrel-Organ*

*a version after Jules Laforgue's "Complainte de l'orgue de Barbarie"*
*followed by an impromptu: "The Organ Grinder's Monkey"*

Barbarous barrel-organ pipes,
Don Quixote on your cart,
cranking out your monkey heart
(while manky guts still squeak and gripe).

All the silly sweaty summers,
sprung from springs so dumb and sober,
to freaky-leaky lockdown October,
then skint in winter. What a bummer!

"The forest falls so hugely still, wet fern
where bloody suns once crashed and burned."

Gaslight, posters, tattered rosters.
Place your bets and raise your bids.
Pianos bang their coffin lids
for tossers, all toupéed imposters.

"Tip-topsily, night is tottering on her way:
all kitten heels and negligée."

Spine-cracked books along the Seine,
wounded shoes in charity shops,
the heel that squeaks or goes *clip-clop*,
crap hats and tat from way back when.

"The park is getting dark, we're lost and scared:
and there's drugged-up muggers, from what I've heard."

Faithful as the earthy veg,
Eve loves him, and that's forever.
And as for us. Nada! Whatever!
She likes to keep us on the edge.

"Corrosive ballets! Is that such a crime?
The moon will pardon me. I won't do time."

Vespers. Raise the golden chalice.
Sunsets. Tribes of Sulamites,
all those whose odd provincial rites
are exiled still by urban malice.

"They've burned me. Left me hopeless as a tramp
dumped in the woods, cold, hungry and damp."

The winds now howl their mournful song,
and there's bugger-all anyone can do.
I cry with the owl: Boo-hoo. Boo-hoo
the whole long, long night long. Night long.

"I'm going to get better. Just look at this scar.
Don't want the hospital. Not going that far."

From the shitty cradle, brother,
to coffins just as vilely bad:
the comfy couples going mad,
ladling soup into one another.

Barbarous barrel-organ pipes,
Don Quixote on your cart,
cranking out your monkey heart,
(while manky guts still squeak and gripe).

## *The Organ Grinder's Monkey*

*impromptu on Jules Laforgue's "Complainte de l'orgue de Barbarie"*

Barbarous, barbarous barrel-organ,
outcranking noise of base degree.
One turns, as from some aural Gorgon's
soul-petrifying machinery.

Wheezy as a drunken carol,
your shit sheet-music's been unstaved:
a chippie chiselled it into the barrel,
and your monkey (got up in panto apparel)
is a wind-up merchant, louche, depraved:
so rude, so rude. – *Oh, do behave!*

Street to street, you map the city,
sniff roasting nuts, horse-piss and dung.
You like the ladies, perfumed and pretty,
slyly stick out your little pink tongue.

Monkey, monkey, manky flunkey,
endlessly on your tin-cup rounds,
almost understanding why,
with your curly tail and dewy eye,
you were born to beg; these sounds
your cue to cheek, be cute and please
(between the scratching at your fleas).

Monkey, monkey, speaking frankly,
grinding your own organ's just going too far.
You're getting rather too rankly wanky.
You're the supporting act and not the star!

You sniff it all. You sniff it all:
the sweat-shop armpits of the poor,
the butcher's meat, the factory's pall,
the beer-breathed toughs, their gin-soaked whores,
the wide-boys with their chivs, the louts.
You sniff it all. You sniff it all.
– All grinding out. All grinding out. –

Monkey in your red velour,
your tiny cap, waistcoat, and chain,
bare your shiny teeth once more
and you'll be beaten once again.

Yes, you'll be beaten once again.

## *Ariadne on Naxos*

*loosely after "Ariane seule" by Marie de Guignes (1862–1907)*

Woke – the sand beneath my cloak was cold.
Stretched out to dawn. You were not there. Ran down
to just your fading sail far out from shore,
day brewing up in the burning blank of sky.

And I was all at sea. Alone. And scared.
I heard the sudden silence of the birds.
And something nearing, thrashing through the scrub.

Cymbals hissed where drumskins shushed those birds.
Then hooves, and hot upon the pad of paws,
strange pelts, immaculately spotted, shone.

Muted by sand, the intermittent wind,
then the sudden advent of that weird band
– all tuning up for opening night tonight
just when I'd thought I'd played and blown my part.

# *Ariadne*

*after "Ariane" by José-Maria de Heredia (1842-1905)*

All bronze and brazen – the din as sun and cymbals clash –
stretched naked along the tiger's back, she catches Bacchus
orchestrating his rag-tag band's slow-motion crash,
as he wheels the monstrous orgy throbbing in his wake.

*The reins fall lightly from her pallid hand.*
*She thrills to the power beneath the pelt, his heat;*
*the beast now snorts, then champs at the flowery bit;*
*retracts his claws, distractedly paws the sand.*

*Her hair falls loose, cascades the roiling flank:*
*gold where amber's zithered by vibrant stripes.*
*Now deaf to the tiger's muted bellow, she's drunk,*
*ecstatic with the god's deep-ripened grapes.*

The lover who fled? Long gone. Nothing left to miss.
The Bride awaits the Conqueror of Asia's kiss.

## *Responses to de Heredia's poem, and Variations on the Theme*

*from* Tigres, et d'autres animaux oniriques

(Tigers and Other Dream Animals)

*poems from an anonymous collaborative sequence privately published around 1905*

After the lost lover, the gate-crashing god
– that much we get. Seems right, and rightly odd.
But her huge tiger? Where did *that* come from?
Suspend all disbelief (though the line's still dumb).

Somewhere else, his *leopards* must have strained
electrically at their harnesses purring through his wine-
soaked retinue of satyrs and fauns:
shaggy-shanked goat-cobbled hoofers and caperers,
the bi-corned and boisterously horny.

But tigers? Is all this Ariadne's dream?
The isle is full of noises, after all.
Who knows what beastly hearts may beat out there,
as he arrives, hurling the curve-ball of himself,
his endless, *da capo*, un-called-for, curtain-call?

*Mme X*

Skirling above the cymbal's brassy crash,
mad music: pipes, that stuff that Plato hated
(rendered us tongueless – ordinarily dumb);
skins flayed and flensed, stretched over the echoing void,
teeth chattering in an ass's jawbone,
the plink of zylophonic ribs. Bone-phone,
moan-phone, skeletal marimba, gonged humerus,
the bag-piped gut or wheezing reed
– and all this mad and maddening crew:
bruisers whose only instrument's a hard-on;
a whole taxonomy of party-animals,
some making mouth-organs of loins, harmonicas of hams,
and others with their hanks of freshly-torn flesh,
very possibly, very possibly, cannibals.

*Mme Y*

## *Parnassian*

Elsewhere, in the *Seizième*, or perhaps
on the low bump of *Montparnasse*, our Poet smokes.
I mean he really *fumes* some aromatic gear.
Think oriental bibelots: silks, *netsuke*,
woodcuts by Utamaro, Hiroshige.
He travels by first editions, his escapes
all lined behind him, Morocco-bound.

In his mind, he's curling waxed moustachios,
with de Montesquiou, or des Esseintes;
his tongue a foil for repartee – a feint,
a parry, and, yes – the point is his – *touché*.
He admires the knotty workmen's muscles
as he lowers the blinds on the world outside;
dreams of women: sensuous, yet classical as marble;
or medievally chaste, a roe-deer nuzzling at this one's sleeve.

Most of all, he imagines abandoning them
to sail into the rose-bright dawn with Ulysses.
He casts a *bon-mot* off. They are too dull to get the joke.
Sometimes, he finds, already abandoned, a maiden
(or is she nymph? a nereid? or maybe maenad?)
implausibly sleeping by a sketchy sea;
then, he quickly shifts, and as she wakes,
our man becomes something utterly else,
something almost fleshed out by wine and smoke.

*Mme Z*

## *Nympholepsy*

*after "La Nympholepsie" by Tristan Branchu (1872–99)*
***Nympholepsy.* *1775.*** *[after epilepsy.] A state of rapture supposed to be inspired in men by nymphs; hence, an ecstasy or frenzy, esp. that caused by desire of the unattainable.* **Shorter Oxford Dictionary***

In the sudden shock of noon
you seek out that bee-loud glade, the low hum
amplified in the fragile vibrato of a flower's drum.
All else is a perfumed narcotic hush:
the sway of big colour on unsteady stems,
each bloom astonishing itself into drunken flame.

You follow the gargle of the river down
to where the breakers tumble hugely in your head;
knowing her wardrobe is racked with tricks of light,
think you have almost glimpsed her gown
in some slight shift of sky or sea.

There, among the dying surf, there's that bright
static foaming through the sand…
– You try to catch her misty hem.
Her sleeve is water in your hand.

Come to – is it moments or is it hours later?
Clothes ragged, slimy, wet;
face stung by salt and sun;
mouth stuffed with weeds and grit;
one low swollen eye
considering a crab scuttling the beach,
a trickle of blood from your nose,
as your mind is pinned by a gull's screech.

***Nympholepsie**: une sorte de folie, de délire fanatique dans lequel les anciens croyoient que tomboit un homme qui avoit aperçu inopinément une Nymphe. (Du grec* numpholepsia, *formé dans la même signification, de* Numphê *Nymphe, et de l'inusité* lêbó *pour* lambanô *je prends, je saisis.)* ***le Dictionnaire de la langue française***

# *Life Model*

*after "La Prisonnière" by Henri de Régnier (1864-1936)*

You're gone, but I caught your eye as you slipped away.
My hand still knows your breast, this curve, that line,
your body's facts are memorised in mine;
I have you studied – drawn, measured, weighed.

Though you've placed the forest and the night
between us, I remember your glow, that spark,
as my mind sketches your chalky form by dark.
I'll refashion you by my studio light.

I'll dress this block, raise you up in stone
to fill the void where you were flesh and bone:
a model inmate, serving Life – lithe

yet mute. How furiously you'll seem to writhe,
so vivaciously dead in marble. – New day,
and already you're a maquette in earthy clay.

## *Offering to Pan*

*after "Offrande à Pan" by Anna de Noailles (1876-1933)*

To this wooden cup, black as an apple pip,
I took the sharp insinuations of my knife;
let folds and frills grow from its sly, bright tip,
until it caught the vine-leaf true to life.

I consecrate my work to Pan, in memory
of the day that Damis snatched it from my hand
– I blushed as that shepherd drank and laughed at me
and impudently stared and stood his ground.

I never found the horned god's altar, so placed
my cup within this cleft of rock right here.
But now my heart thirsts for the lasting taste
of that deep kiss... and something's moving near.

## *Parthenon Bas-Relief*

*after "Celle qui passe: bas-relief du Parthénon" by Gérard d'Houville (1875-1963), pseudonym of Marie de Régnier, née Marie Louise Antoinette de Heredia. The bas-relief is* Nike Adjusting her Sandal *(c. 410 BCE), a fragment from the Temple of Athena Nike at the Acropolis. The sculpture is damaged and Nike, winged goddess of victory, has no face.*

**The Passer-by**

An age away you stopped to tie your lace.
What was your name? Who traced your frozen charm?
Your body's with us still: you have no face.

Was it soft, or haughty? Tender, fearful, calm?
We'll never know if it equalled the way your stance
tips a half-cradled breast from your folded arm.

Forever you twist to retie your sandal, balanced,
one foot in air, gathering up your train,
a fugitive caught in a pale marble trance.

Where are you from? Which god awaits in vain?
You can no longer hurry on. You remain
here, beyond all happiness and pain.

You were so ready, always already gone.
You rest alert, eyes neither open nor shut,
sleep rippling your tunic of diaphanous stone.

Time to let go that cloth's now useless knot.
One arrives too soon among the Shades.
Your headstone's dressed: your dates already cut.

Heading to Hades or the sexton's spade,
why bother, girl, to up your game, unfreeze?
That sculptor saw your body open wide

and caught it hinged on the springs of your young knees
Listen! Just stay like that. Old age, disease,
they lie in wait. These things and more besides.

Best now to pause, now everything's in place.
Death will surely come. I know. I know.
No longer any need to see your face.

I think... I think... I think it looks like Grace.

**Nike Tying Her Sandal**

Minutes or millennia later, she's all wound up,
crouched to check her laces. Tick.
Fits spikes to block, coiled and ready.

Gone. Already, long, long gone.
Cracked her getaway, left us
with the dying echo from the gun.

## *Fabrication*

*very loosely after "Faste des tissus" by Renée Vivien (1877-1909)*

To slant rhymes obliquely with your clothes,
mix verse with assonantal prose.

Experiment with genre, persona, mode;
wear sonnet, lyric and formal ode.

Swish to the rhythm of fashionable tides:
cover the linen of girls, the passion of brides.

A chasuble stitched with violet and gold
finds incense scenting each secret fold.

O ocean nymphs, your flashing eyes
are foam-flecked lace under azure skies.

Let the heavy fall of velvet copy
the reveries of the drowsy poppy.

Cold satin may deceive the eye,
or shimmer to suggest warm thighs.

Raise your cheek up to be kissed
in lacy hoarfrost, embroidered mist.

Old lilies lie, all choked by fronds;
fresh watered silk's your glittering pond.

Your wise immodesty deserves all praise:
let minstrels sing the lady's Lays.

And what is more is often less:
severe restraint, that little black dress.

Cut on the bias. O pinking mavericks,
let me see you slash those fabrics.

Supermodel, catwalk thin:
all Vogue on the outside, vague on the in.

Reveries of navy, turquoise, rose:
clothes suppler than verse, more solemn than prose.

## *The Cemetery by the Sea*

*after Paul Valéry (1871-1945): "Le Cimetière marin"*

*"My soul, do not strive for immortality, but make the most of what is practicable"*
*– Pindar, Pythian Odes III*

This peaceful roof, its tombs in long buckled lines...
As noon performs its daily alchemy,
doves flicker up from stones through tall blue pines.
And I am here. All this now glows for me:
the sea, the sea, once more transformed by fire;
a moment's calm, beyond small wants, desire.

What pure work of graceful light now roams
the vastness of the sea. Its darts consume
detail: scattered diamonds gleam in foam
as the dark abyss is slowly tipped by sun.
Time scintillates and suddenly it seems
knowledge descends like a lucid dream.

Unchanging treasure, shrine to wise Minerva,
great rock of calm and visible reserve.
Below that eye, proud water, somnolent, ample;
power, asleep beneath its veil of fire.
My silence grows within this simple temple,
its pinnacle of gold, its ancient spire.

Temple of time, its sum a single sigh.
I climb the heights where distance blunts the gaze
– the way, up here, the sea surrounds the eye
where broadcast seeds of light now dull to haze,
an offering as sea shifts blue to green
that casts disdain on what is merely seen.

And just as eaten fruit melts into taste
where tongue finds solid form has left no trace,
so absence may be transformed into delight.
I breathe the smoke I shall become, the light,
while sky now sings its song consumed by fire,
echoing the restless murmuring shore.

Beneath that light-charged sky, look how I change!
After so much pride, so much that's strange,
so full of sloth, yet full of new-born power,
I give myself up to this brilliant space.
On the houses of the dead, I see my shadow pass
– how ephemeral and frail the body's hour.

I'll have my soul exposed to solstice torches,
to bear the solar justice of the light.
Your pitilessly shining weapons pierce and scorch;
I return your honours, all the highest grade.
You glow with pride, but to reflect that bright
midday implies a half of mournful shade.

For me alone, within myself, unbent,
I see, beside the heart, the poem's source
between the emptiness and pure event,
awaiting the presage of an inner grandeur:
a dark and bitter echoing well – a hole,
a void forever ringing in the soul.

Do you know, fake captive of the leaves,
this bone-filled ground? What knotted brow conceived
this greedy gulf devouring the railing's bars?
The mysteries we screen behind closed eyes?
The pull of indolence, the will's demise?
The spark evoking all those loved and lost?

Holy enclosure filled with abstract fire,
an earthly fragment offered up to light,
in thrall to these perversely solid pyres
– torches of gold or stone; dark poplar flames –
where so much marble trembles over shade,
the faithful sea asleep where your body's laid.

Tethered, the sea growls off idolaters while,
all alone with just a shepherd's smile,
I tend my flock of grazing sepulchres,
hear its boom banish the anxious birds
as it churns to ward off hopeless dreams, avert
from whitened tombs the angels' prying eyes.

Once here, the future lies in idleness.
The insect scratches at the bone-dry soil.
This world's burned up, fugitive, turned to air,
into I know not what austere essence.
Life is vast and drunk on its own absence:
its bitterness is sweet; the mind is clear.

The dead lie easy, hidden in this soil
which warms and dries their unsolved mystery.
Up there, midday: the motionless noon-time boils,
imagined into self-sufficiency,
the regal head that bears the perfect crown.
I am within you; each secret change my own.

You have only me to hold your fears.
Repentence, doubts, constraints, my servile mind:
I see the same flaws in your vaunted diamond.
At night, so heavy with statuary and marble,
right down in the roots of trees, a shadowy people
declares itself for you, and all your kind.

They have melted into a dense absence.
Red clay has drunk them dry, drained every sense;
their gift of life had fled into the flowers.
Where are their turns of phrase, these distant dead?
Their singular arts, their souls, long praised by peers?
The grubs now thread their way where once were tears.

The shrill and tickled girls with piercing cries:
their teeth, their moist eyelids, their flashing eyes;
the blood which throbs within those bee-stung lips;
the fingers which defend those hidden favours.
Soft skin, soft breasts – oh how we burned with lust –
return to earth. All flesh is grass. Is dust.

And you, great soul, are you waiting for a dream
with colours true to life, which never lies?
– One made for eyes of flesh by wave and gold?
Will you still sing when you are thinnest air?
Those dreams, like life, are fleeting, soon grow old.
And even holy patience also dies.

This immortality of black and gold,
hideous consoler wreathed with laurel
who makes of grinning death a mother's breast
– a pretty fiction and a pious ruse.
Who does not know, and who would not refuse
its mocking laughter, that empty skull's old jest?

You lie so deep, my fathers, your abandoned heads
accustomed to the weight of earth in spades,
the ground we limp upon, unsure, infirm.
The gnawing truth, the irrefutable worm
is not for you who sleep beneath the slab.
Its peace lives on in me and never fades.

Is it love, perhaps? Self-hatred buried deep?
What secret tooth could lie as close as his now seems?
He may go by any name or none,
no matter, he sees and wishes, touches, dreams.
My flesh is to his taste, he haunts my sleep.
My constant shadow, through me he still lives on.

O Zeno with your Zen-like paradox,
you pierce me perversely with your logic's arrow
– the one that flies but never leaves the bow:
think Schrödinger's cat, in the limbo of its box,
undead; Achilles slowed to a tortoise-shadow.
Uncertainty: the principle we'll never know.

Enough! Get up, confront this coming age.
Break, my body, from out your pensive cage
and fill your lungs, drink in that vital wind,
harness its salty power, fresh from the sea.
I breathe in deep. My soul returns. Fresh-skinned,
I run into the waves. Reborn. Leap free.

Go crashing those ecstatic roiling peaks
with panther skin, like some heroic Greek,
my tunic full of the sun's repeated disk
– drunk on my own blue flesh, that thrilling risk
the wild beast knows, unawed by death or violence,
in a tumult of spray eloquent as silence.

The wind is rising. It's time to seize my life.
The burly air is rifling through my book,
bullies nervous pages, shoos reading off.
Break waves! Fly pages! Feel elements in joyful strife.
Waves burst, explode in light and spray from the rocks.
Sails nod the tide, bob white where they peck like doves.

## *Bestiary*

*after Guillaume Apollinaire (1880–1918). Excerpts from Apollinaire's first book* Le Bestiare ou cortège d'Orphée *(1911), which was illustrated by celebrated woodcuts by Raoul Dufy*

### Orpheus

He cuts a powerful and fine
figure from a noble line.
He steps from shade; he has no peer:
his voice shines Light upon the ear.

### Tortoise

The beasts approached to hear me sing;
my fingers danced upon the strings.
In magic Thrace, they knew me well,
loved songs I conjured up from shell.

### Horse

Through the exercise of endless pains,
my formal dreams shall act as reins.
I'll master you: my Will be done
– we'll save the gallop till we are one.

### Mouse

The days beat as fast as your little chest,
already the summer's past its best.
You weight the corn, bend it to your paw,
pause a moment, then *gnaw*, *gnaw*, *gnaw*.

## Lion

O Lion, once such a noble king,
your mane's all mangy now – Poor thing!
Cat got your tongue? Where is your roar, your rage?
Cut down to size. Born in a cage.

## Fly

Odd, that our flies still know
those songs they learned in Norway.
Seems French flies remain always
divinities of snow.

## Jellyfish

Medusas with your saddened heads
haloed by your ultra-violet hair,
you make the storm-tossed sea your happy bed.
Me too! I guess we make a pair.

## Snake

You've got an eye for beauty.
God! How many women have there been?
Eve, Eurydice, Cleo. All victims of your cruelty.
The three or four I've known personally,
the hundreds more I've seen.

# *Notes*

Several of these poets are fictitious. They include Mmes X, Y and Z responding to de Heredia, and the following:

**Marie de Guignes (1862-1907)** Mistress to several politicians and artists.

**Tristan Branchu (1872-99)** Opium addict.

This is an essentially personal take on some French poets from the mid-nineteenth century to the First World War. I have chosen poems I like and felt I could turn into English versions or work interesting variations on. One or two major poets, such as Victor Hugo, are missing. Hugo doesn't quite fit into the arc I'm suggesting. The narrative I trace, starting with Gautier, has Romanticism morphing into Symbolism and its subsequent decadence; this in turn gives way to the energy of an Apollinaire using the dressing-up box of history to predict the wardrobe of the future as Symbolism becomes, inevitably, through its self-conscious aesthetic awareness, the nurse of Modernism.

I have taken some liberties with the usual chronological order of poets in the interests of thematic or stylistic continuity or contrast. Corbière, though writing before Rimbaud, seems more naturally to precede Laforgue. Likewise, as de Heredia's 118 collected sonnets were not published until 1893, under the title *Les Trophées*, and the responses to his poem by other poets included here follow this date, I have placed him considerably later in the selection than is the usual case in anthologies.

Liberties have also been taken with the conventions of capitalising the initial letter of verse lines. This has occasionally been preserved to indicate a classical form such as the often ubiquitous French alexandrines (though I have often tended to anglicise these into pentameters). Elsewhere I have often ignored capitalisation where I felt the verse was moving towards something freer in terms of metre, tone or effect and retained it when it seemed to nod to the conventions of folk-lyric. There is, however, no hard and fast distinction; I've treated each poem in terms of how I felt it best worked in English.

## *Acknowledgements:*

Some of these poems, or earlier versions of them, appeared in or on: *The Common* online (Amherst, USA); *The French Literary Review*; the Grierson Centre, University of Aberdeen https://griersoncentre.wordpress.com/poetry/; *Stand*; *Strange Tongues* (Weasel Productions); *Trans* (The Collective Press, Wales); *Tupelo Quarterly* (online). Two Laforgue versions appeared in *All Keyboards are Legitimate*, ed. Suzannah V. Evans (Guillemot Press, 2023). Thanks also to CAMAC (Centre d'art Marnay-sur-Seine) and the University of Hull who jointly funded the residency in France during which I started this project.

***French Leave*** is a sort of companion volume to ***RE:VERB*** (Broken Sleep, 2022), which includes variations on themes in Rimbaud's ***Une Saison en Enfer*** and a verse biography based on his travels and particularly his letters from Africa.

LAY OUT YOUR UNREST

www.ingramcontent.com/pod-product-compliance
Lightning Source LLC
La Vergne TN
LVHW051017080826
845145LV00009B/2674